DINING W
LIYUEN

35 years of memories and Chinese recipes

Copyright

Dining with Liyuen: 35 Years of memories and Chinese recipes

Published by Piscataqua Press
An imprint of RiverRun Bookstore
142 Fleet St., Portsmouth, NH 03801

www.ppressbooks.com
www.riverrunbookstore.com

ISBN: 978-1-939739-84-1

Printed in the United States of America

DINING WITH LIYUEN

35 years of memories and Chinese recipes

Liyuen Buesing

photos by
Kindra Clineff

foreword by
Senator Judd Gregg

Contents

Contents

Foreword

Liyuen's Chinese Culinary Specialties has been a favorite of our entire family for years. Her emphasis on locally sourced food and her enthusiastic support for small businesses in the Seacoast exemplify her as a community-minded citizen.

The impact Liyuen has had over the past 35 years is enormous. Thousands of students have attended her cooking classes, and countless meals shared by families from her catering and carry-out. She always greets her customers with a warm smile and calls them by name, and the holiday card and picture 'Wall of Fame' in her store represents the highly personal experience that she is famous for.

Her cookbook, Dining with Liyuen, is another milestone in an accomplished career. Anyone who has had the pleasure of meeting Liyuen or sampled her delicious food will treasure this book and enjoy reading the stories that accompany each recipe. She has truly redefined what we've come to expect from Chinese cuisine in New Hampshire.

Senator Judd Gregg

Introduction

My career as a Chinese cooking instructor began in 1981 in my home kitchen in Rye, NH. Four of my girlfriends asked if I could share with them how to make a couple of simple recipes. They raved about the experience and encouraged me to teach them more recipes. I realized there was an appetite in the Seacoast area for learning the art of Chinese cooking, and I saw an opportunity to pass on a piece of my culture from Taiwan. Word quickly spread of my in-home cooking school, and soon there were so many cars in our driveway that the neighbors began to complain. I knew it was time to move to a real commercial space. With very little knowledge of how to operate a start-up business, I opened Liyuen's Chinese Culinary Specialties in downtown Portsmouth, NH in 1987. The response was overwhelmingly positive, and in 1993, I expanded to North Hampton, NH, adding a carry-out counter in our new space. None of this would have been possible without my dear friend and early business partner, Mara Khavari, who provided financial support, and a handful of close friends who guided me on how to set up shop, apply for a bank loan, purchase equipment, and do all of the other things that make a business successful.

With my mother, 1991

Teaching in my Portsmouth shop, 1988

It has truly been a privilege to serve the Seacoast community. I have absolutely loved teaching students the art of traditional Chinese cooking, getting to know all of my customers personally, and working with the local markets and health food stores that have carried our spring rolls and noodle salads. I feel incredibly blessed with all of your support.

When I first mentioned to my family that it was perhaps time for me to retire, they encouraged me to write a cookbook, which had always been on my bucket list. The result is a collection of the most popular recipes from my cooking classes, catering, and carry-out, accompanied by a short narrative of why I included each one. I would like to thank my son Eric, daughter-in-law Arpita, and nieces Jennifer and Janet for encouraging me to write this book. They worked as tirelessly as I did to edit my stories and refine my recipes so that I could share them with the Seacoast community.

You're gonna love it!

Liyuen

Making spring rolls in North Hampton, 1995

Thirty-five years and still cooking! 2015

Unique Ingredients

Many of the dishes in my cookbook call for unique Chinese ingredients. You can usually find them in Asian markets, health food stores, and even in the Asian section of many grocery stores. These days, you may even order many of these ingredients over the Internet! In some cases, alternatives or substitutes can be used, which I have highlighted below and in the recipes.

Arrowroot

Many of my dishes call for arrowroot for marinating, sealing pastes, or thickener for sauces. I prefer it as a thickener over cornstarch because it is healthier and has a more neutral flavor for delicate sauces. Always mix arrowroot with a little water in a dish to make a blended slurry before adding it to your dishes as a thickener. Cornstarch or potato flour can also be used as a substitute.

Chicken stock

Chicken stock is the base for many of my recipes. Store bought chicken stock can always be used, but I prefer to make a fresh chicken stock and then freeze it in small containers until I need it. To make a simple stock, add a whole chicken or large package of chicken legs (approximately 3-5 pounds) to a large pot and fill ¾ full of cold water. Bring to a boil, reduce heat and cover. Cook the stock for about 2 hours. Remove the chicken with tongs (this chicken meat can be used for other dishes like salads) and strain out any large pieces or solids from the stock. Bring the stock back to a rolling boil and cook uncovered for another 10-15 minutes to reduce down to a rich stock. When the stock has finished reducing, allow it to rest until the excess fat forms a layer on top of the stock. Skim off with a ladle and discard the fat. The stock can be stored in an airtight container in the refrigerator for about a week, or it can be frozen for a few months.

Chinese brown peppercorn

Sometimes known as Sichuan pepper or Chinese coriander, Chinese brown peppercorn can be found in Asian markets and many health food stores. Black peppercorn can be used as a substitute.

Chinese five-spice powder

While there are many variations on five-spice powder, usually it is a blend of star anise, cloves, cinnamon, Sichuan pepper, and fennel seed. Outside of Asian markets, it can often be found in many grocery stores.

Dried red chilli peppers

This is a staple ingredient in Sichuan cooking. Dried chillies come in different varieties and levels of spiciness. You can find them in Asian markets, health food stores, and in some grocery stories.

Unique Ingredients

Dried wood ear mushrooms

Sometimes known as black fungus, wood ear mushrooms have a firm skin with slightly crunchy texture.

Hot pepper oil (chilli oil)

Chinese hot pepper oil adds a rich spiciness and deep red color to dishes. You can find it Asian markets and most grocery stores.

Monosodium glutamate (MSG)

Traditional Chinese dishes often call for the use of MSG, which is a flavor enhancer like salt. I've always believed that in small quantities, MSG is not bad for you, and it really does enhance the flavor of many dishes. I understand that some people prefer not to use MSG, so it is listed as optional in some recipes.

Mung bean noodles

Sometimes called cellophane noodle or bean thread noodles, mung bean noodles are thin vermicelli made from mung bean flour. They are generally sold in dried form.

Oyster sauce

This is a thick dark brown condiment made from sugar and salt, and flavored with a little oyster essence. You can usually find this in your local grocery store.

Rice (short-grain)

Many of the dishes in this cookbook are best served over cooked rice. I prefer high-quality short-grain white rice that is cooked in a rice cooker or in a pot on the stove.

Rice sticks (dried rice noodles)

Rice sticks (or dried rice noodles) are semi-transparent noodles found in Asian markets and most grocery stores. Some are thin like angel hair pasta, other varieties are thick like linguini.

Rice wine

Rice wine is a staple in Chinese cooking, particularly for marinades to enhance the flavor of meats, poultry, and fish. It can be found in Asian markets or in the Asian section of local grocery stores. Pale dry sherry wine can be used as a substitute.

Sesame oil

Asian sesame oil has a rich dark color and intense aroma. I use it to add flavor and fragrance to many dishes and sauces.

Sesame paste (sesame seed paste)

Sesame paste is made from sesame seeds, and has the consistency of peanut butter. You can find it in Asian markets and many grocery stores. Some health food stores call it tahini paste.

Soy sauce

This is an essential seasoning in Chinese cooking. Both light or dark soy sauce can be used in these recipes, but generally I use light soy sauce with lower sodium for sauces, and dark soy sauce when marinating.

Spring roll and wonton wrappers

Wrappers for making spring rolls and wontons can be found in Asian markets and many grocery stores. Spring roll wrappers are thinner and larger, about the size of a square sheet of paper. Wonton wrappers are thicker and about the size of a square coaster.

Star anise

This dried spice resembles a star with dark brown pods that contain pea-sized seeds. It has a distinct and wonderful sweet licorice aroma and flavor.

Tofu

You can find tofu in almost every grocery store. Generally I like to use firm tofu because it holds up better when cooking, however for certain dishes like Ma Po Tofu, I prefer a soft, silken tofu.

Equipment I Use in the Kitchen

Just as having the right ingredients is essential for ensuring an authentic flavor, using the right equipment really makes the dish.

Asian wok

A good wok is an essential component of Chinese cooking. Using a wok allows you to stir-fry and toss the ingredients vigorously over high heat with less oil. To make cooking on your home stove easier, try using a stainless steel, flat-bottomed wok. A large frying pan can be used as a substitute.

Chinese ladle

I always use a stainless steel ladle. It is longer and sturdier than a Western spatula with less of an angle between the handle and shovel, making it ideal for stir-frying in a wok.

Electric rice cooker

A rice cooker is an essential appliance in my kitchen. It is simple to use: just measure the rice and water, press a single button, and your rice is cooked perfectly and kept hot until ready to serve.

Steamer

Some of the dishes call for steaming. Either a bamboo or metal steamer placed in a wok or large covered pot of water can be used.

Liyuen's Famous Spring Rolls

(Approximately 24 rolls)

My Spring Rolls started my whole business 35 years ago. At that time, I was disappointed at what I call the "E-G-G" rolls being served in local Chinese restaurants. Not only did they not taste like what I remembered and loved from my childhood in Taiwan, but I also knew them to be called "Spring Rolls" because there was no egg in how I had learned to make them.

After hearing from family and friends about how different my Spring Rolls tasted, I taught a few people how to make them at our home in Rye, NH. Over the next 35 years, these spring rolls became a favorite in our carry-out and found their way into hundreds of fresh markets and health food stores across the New England seacoast. By my estimate, I've sold over 1 million, every single one made with my own hands.

This recipe for Liyuen's Spring Rolls is unchanged from what I taught in my home kitchen all those years ago. To this day, I still enjoy eating these spring rolls, and they are requested at every family occasion. I know you will enjoy making, eating and sharing these as well.

Marinade
4 Tbs. soy sauce
1 Tbs. arrowroot
⅛ tsp. Chinese five-spice powder

Filling
6 pcs. dried shiitake mushrooms
2 oz. mung bean noodles
8 oz. pork (sliced into thin strips)
4 Tbs. water
4 Tbs. oil
1 tsp. salt
1 cup carrots (shredded)
1 cup celery (shredded)
1 cup scallion (shredded)
1 pkg. spring roll wrappers
3 cups vegetable oil for frying

Sealing paste
Mix 1 heaping Tbs. flour with 1 Tbs. water

Continued on next page...

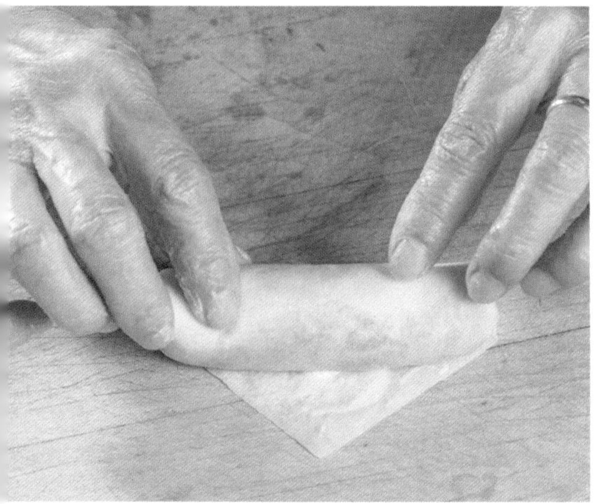

1. Soak the mung bean noodles in warm water for 5–10 minutes until they are soft.
2. Soak dried mushrooms in warm water for 45–60 minutes, until softened. Fresh shiitake mushrooms can also be used, rinsed clean. Shred the mushrooms. Cut noodles in 2-inch lengths.
3. In a bowl, combine marinade sauce ingredients and mix well. Add pork to the bowl, mix well, and set aside.
4. In a wok or large frying pan, heat 3 Tbs. vegetable oil over high heat until hot, sauté marinated pork for approximately 2 minutes, then remove.
5. In the same wok or large frying pan, heat 1 Tbs. vegetable oil over high heat until hot, turn heat low and add mung bean noodles, shredded mushrooms, 4 Tbs. water and salt. Mix and cook for about 2 minutes. Add carrots, celery and mix well. Add the marinated pork and cook until evenly heated (approximately 2–3 minutes). Add scallions and cook until hot and remove from heat.
6. Transfer cooked filling to a large bowl and let cool to room temperature.
7. Combine sealing paste ingredients into a small dish.
8. Place 2 Tbs. of cooled filling on a single spring roll wrapper (approximately 2 inches from the corner nearest to you). Roll one complete turn, fold right and left sides in toward center and continue rolling up tight. Using the tip of your finger, spread a bit of sealing paste to seal closed.
9. Heat 3 cups of vegetable oil in a medium sized pot. Deep fry spring rolls using high heat (350°F), for approximately 2 minutes, or until golden brown.
10. Remove and let cool for a few minutes before serving. Best served with sweet & sour sauce (duck sauce).

Optional: A vegetarian version of this recipe can be made by substituting wheat meat instead of pork.

Crab Rangoon

(Makes 30–50 pieces)

This recipe came about after I visited a local Chinese restaurant with some friends many years ago. When I tasted the restaurant's version of crab rangoon, I noticed that it was made with artificial crab meat and too much cream cheese. Right then I knew that if I were to create a crab rangoon recipe, it would have to include real crab meat balanced with the right amount of cream cheese, and reinforced with traditional Asian flavors of scallion and cilantro.

Our crab rangoons are loved by locals all over New England. I will always remember one customer from Manchester, VT who would drive all the way to the Seacoast and never leave without ordering these.

Filling

½ lb. fresh cooked crabmeat
½ lb. cream cheese
2 Tbs. scallion (chopped)
2 Tbs. cilantro (chopped)
1 package wonton wrappers (thin)
3 cups vegetable oil for frying

Sealing paste

Mix 1 heaping Tbs. flour with 1 Tbs. water

1. Squeeze excess water out of crabmeat (the drier the better).
2. In a large bowl, combine crabmeat, cream cheese, scallion and cilantro.
3. Combine sealing paste ingredients into a small dish.
4. Scoop 1 teaspoon of filling onto the center of a wrapper. Bring all 4 corners together and brush inside edges with a tiny bit of sealing paste to close.
5. Heat 3 cups of vegetable oil in a medium pot. Deep fry crab rangoons using high heat (325°F), for approximately 1 minute, or until lightly browned.
6. Remove and let cool for a few minutes before serving.

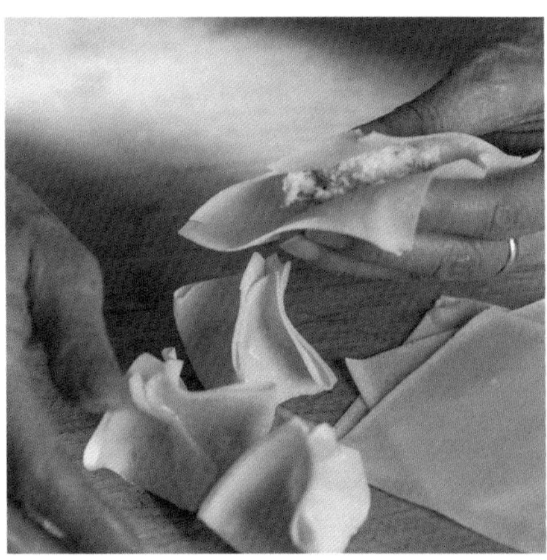

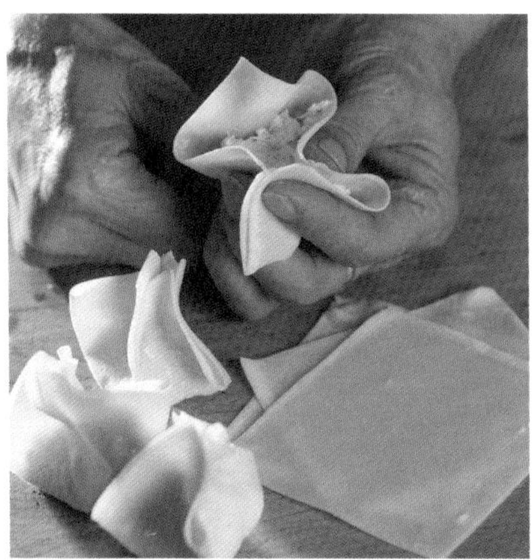

Scallion Pancake

(Approximately 3 pancakes)

One of my favorite foods from the Shandong province is scallion pancakes. I absolutely loved eating them growing up! After coming to the United States, I noticed that no one made scallion pancakes the way I had seen them made in Taiwan. I wanted to teach my students the traditional way of making scallion pancakes. The dough is mixed with scallions and then stretched and folded over and over again, making many thin layers, and then the pancake is lightly pan fried. This method creates a crisp outer skin, with layer upon layer of soft flavorful pancake on the inside. I taught my staff how to make these the way I learned to growing up, and to this day we still hand-make every single scallion pancake sold in our carry-out.

Pancake dough
2 cups flour
⅔ cup very hot water

Scallion mixture
2 Tbs. scallion (diced very fine)
3 Tbs. lard or shortening
½ tsp. salt
6 Tbs. vegetable oil for pan frying

Continued on next page...

...continued.

1. Slowly mix very hot water into flour and knead dough very well until smooth with no lumps, being careful not to burn yourself. If dough is too dry, then add a few drops of cold water. Cover dough with a damp cloth or plastic wrap and set aside for 15 minutes.

2. Make scallion mixture and set aside.

3. Knead dough until very smooth and separate dough into 3 equal parts. Using a rolling pin, roll each part into a large, thin pancake.

4. Add approximately 1 Tbs. of scallion mixture on top of each pancake and spread evenly.

5. Starting on one end, first roll up each pancake into a long tube, then roll each pancake again sideways into a snail shape. Rolled pancakes can be either set aside in the refrigerator until ready to cook or frozen.

6. Using a rolling pin or your hands, press down to flatten pancake and roll out to approximately an 8-inch-round circle.

7. In a frying pan, heat 2 Tbs. vegetable oil until hot on medium/high heat. Place pancake in pan and cook for approximately 1–2 minutes and flip over to fry other side for an additional 1–2 minutes. Flip a couple of times to ensure even cooking on both sides until done. Make sure both sides are nicely browned.

8. Remove from heat and set aside for a few minutes to cool. Cut each pancake into pieces before serving. Repeat this procedure for remaining pancakes.

Pan Fried Pork Dumplings

(Approximately 35–40 pieces)

A beloved symbol of prosperity, dumplings are a staple in the Chinese diet. In the northern provinces, they are often served boiled, while in the southern parts of China, such as Shanghai, they are often pan fried. While there are many different varieties of dumplings including cabbage, garlic chives, and different types of meat, I prefer a traditional pan fried dumpling made with ground pork and scallions.

Making dumplings together is a fun activity that the whole family can enjoy. Nothing compares to a handmade dumpling from scratch. I always make the wrapper very thin so it highlights the flavor of the filling. However, store-bought wrappers will work as well. Always make a few extra because once you serve them they won't last long!

Dough
3½ cups flour
1½ cups very hot water
2 Tbs. vegetable oil

Filling
1 lb. ground pork
8 oz. cabbage (chopped)
1 tsp. ginger root (chopped)
½ cup scallion (chopped)
3 Tbs. soy sauce
2 Tbs. sesame oil
1 tsp. honey
1 egg
2 Tbs. arrowroot (can be substituted with cornstarch)
½ tsp. salt

Sauce for dipping (may be doubled)
3 Tbs. soy sauce
1 Tbs. rice vinegar
1 tsp. sesame oil
1 tsp. honey
½ tsp. ginger root (minced)

Continued on next page...

...continued.

1. Slowly mix very hot water into flour and knead dough very well until smooth with no lumps, being careful not to burn yourself. If dough is too dry, then add a few drops of cold water (the dough should resemble the consistency of pie crust). Cover with cloth and set dough aside for 10–15 minutes.

2. Combine filling ingredients in a large bowl and mix until very smooth.

3. Dust a cutting board or clean countertop with flour. Place dough on top and continue to knead until smooth.

4. Roll dough into a long tube and cut dough into 35–40 pieces, each 1½ inches long. Using your hand, flatten each piece into a 3-inch-round pancake.

5. Add 1 Tbs. of filling in the center of dough. Fold into half circle and snap the edges together (use a little water on your finger as necessary to seal the dough edges together).

6. In a large frying pan add 1 Tbs. vegetable oil and ½ cup water. Line up the dumplings neatly in a single layer and cover. Pan fry dumplings over medium-low heat until bottoms are nice and browned (about 15 minutes).

7. Remove from heat. Repeat the same procedure for remaining dumplings.

Sichuan Cold Cucumber Salad

(4–6 servings)

When I was young I did not always love spicy food, but my mother, being from Sichuan province, cooked with chilli all the time. We learned quickly that if we didn't come to like spicy food, we were going to go hungry! Once I learned to appreciate spicy food, my palate was opened up to a world of wonderful dishes.

I love this dish because it's healthy, enticing, and so quick and easy to make. You can eat it without any guilt! It's the perfect appetizer or side dish, but I can happily eat it as a meal by itself.

1½ lbs. small cucumbers (pickling cukes)
1 Tbs. hot pepper oil
1 Tbs. salt

Sauce
2 cloves garlic (diced)
1 Tbs. rice vinegar
1 tsp. honey
2 tsp. sesame oil
⅛ tsp. MSG (optional)

1. Cut cucumbers into rectangular slices, approximately 2 inches in length. Mix with salt and set aside for 30 minutes to 1 hour.
2. Rinse cucumber lightly with water and pat dry with paper towels to remove excess water.
3. In a small bowl, combine sauce ingredients, add cucumbers and mix thoroughly. Add hot pepper oil to finish and stir.
4. Place salad in refrigerator and serve chilled. Best if done one day ahead.

Hot and Sour Soup

(6–8 servings)

Many of my students tell me that they judge the quality of a Chinese restaurant by the hot and sour soup, since it's served in almost every Chinese restaurant. We have customers who travel from all over New England for our hot and sour soup, and of course they always say ours is the best!

While this is probably the most commonly available soup in Chinese restaurants, not all hot and sour soup recipes are the same. Ours is a traditional recipe that originates from the northeastern region of China. It was taught to me by my mother. What makes this recipe stand out is the freshness and quality of the traditional ingredients we use, including homemade chicken soup stock.

Soup

1 oz. dried tiger lilies (daylily stems) (Canned bamboo shoots cut into long thin strips can be used in the absence of daylily stems)
¼ oz. dried wood ear mushrooms
6 cups chicken soup stock (see Unique Ingredients section)
½ Tbs. salt
2 Tbs. soy sauce
2 Tbs. vinegar
4 oz. tofu (cut into thin strips)
1 tsp. hot pepper oil
1 tsp. white pepper
1 egg (beaten)

Marinated pork

4 oz. pork loin (sliced into thin strips)
1 Tbs. soy sauce
1 tsp. arrowroot (can be substituted with cornstarch)

Soup thickening mix

½ cup chicken soup stock
3 Tbs. arrowroot (can be substituted with cornstarch)

1. Soak tiger lilies and wood ear mushrooms in warm water until softened. Rinse thoroughly and shred.
2. Make marinated pork by mixing shredded pork with soy sauce and arrowroot.
3. Mix soup thickening ingredients and set aside.
4. In a large pot, bring chicken soup stock to a boil, add salt, tiger lilies, wood ear mushrooms, soy sauce and vinegar and stir. Boil for approximately 5 minutes.
5. Turn heat down to medium and add marinated pork. Slowly add soup thickening mix and tofu, stirring slowly until thickened.
6. Add hot pepper oil and white pepper. Turn heat to very low.
7. Slowly drizzle egg into soup while stirring, turn heat off, then let set.

Egg Drop Soup

(6–8 servings)

This is traditionally an appetizer soup popular in China and Taiwan and in the U.S. It is called egg drop because you slowly trickle a beaten egg into chicken soup stock on the stove until the drops of egg quickly cook and float to the surface.

The secret to a better egg drop soup is to make a rich chicken stock from scratch and thicken it slightly with arrowroot. The soup is finished off with a drizzle of sesame oil and chopped scallions for flavor.

I always make a large batch of homemade chicken stock and store it in containers in the freezer because it's the base of so many dishes. That way, making egg drop soup can be done in only a few minutes.

6 cups chicken soup stock
(see Unique Ingredients section)
2 eggs (beaten)
2 Tbs. scallion (diced)
2 tsp. sesame oil
3 Tbs. arrowroot (can be
substituted with cornstarch)
4 Tbs. water
½ Tbs. salt

1. In a large pot, bring chicken soup stock to a boil.
2. Mix arrowroot with water until dissolved. Pour slowly into lightly boiling soup stock and add salt.
3. Stir soup until thickened, approximately 1 minute.
4. Slowly drizzle eggs into the soup while stirring constantly.
5. Turn heat off and add scallions.
6. Pour soup into serving bowl and sprinkle sesame oil on top just before serving.

Wonton Soup

(6–8 servings)

The first Chinese people to migrate to U.S. were mostly Cantonese, and they called a seasoned pork filling in a thin wrapper, wontons. In Taiwan, we called these huntun. When I first made these wontons for my students in the 1980s, everyone commented on how different they were. They can be served fried as an appetizer or cooked in stock for wonton soup, which is my favorite way to prepare them. Today my son loves to make these, and he teaches his family and friends how to make them too.

This recipe calls for a simple and delicate chicken soup stock made from scratch that is pleasing to the palate and complements the rich flavor of the wontons. Combine these with a little spinach for a wonderful soup your whole family will love.

Filling

1 lb. ground pork
1 egg (beaten)
1 Tbs. arrowroot (can be substituted with cornstarch)
2 tsp. sesame oil
½ tsp. salt
½ tsp. white pepper
1 package wonton wrappers (thin)

Soup

6–8 cups chicken soup stock (see Unique Ingredients section)
2 Tbs. scallion (diced)
½ Tbs. salt

1. In a large bowl, combine ground pork, egg, arrowroot, sesame oil, salt, and white pepper, and mix thoroughly until thickened.
2. Using a small spoon, put approximately 1 tsp. of filling in corner of wonton wrapper closest to you. Fold wrapper just over filling and fold again. Using your finger dipped in water, slightly wet the left and right tip of the wrapper and pinch ends together to seal, forming a triangular shape. Repeat until all the wontons have been made.
3. Bring soup to a boil in a large pot, add wontons (3-4 per person) and salt. Cook for 5 minutes.
4. Remove from heat and add scallions.

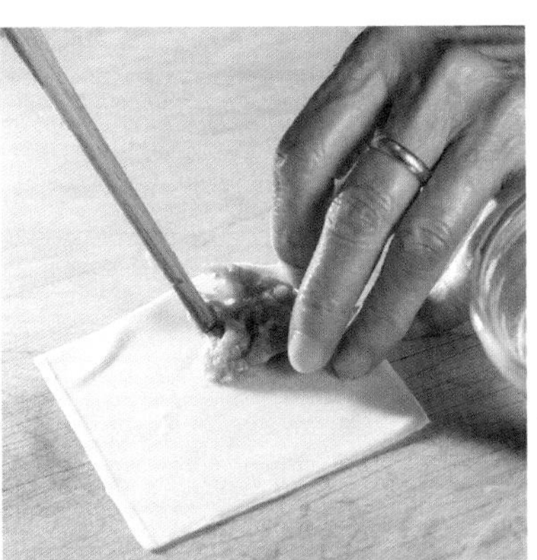

Stewed Beef Noodle Soup

(6–8 large servings)

This 'meal portion' soup is famous in Taiwan. I used to take a bus almost an hour each way to go from my college campus in Yangmingshan to a restaurant in Taipei city that was famous for this soup. It is so popular and loved by all that there are contests for the best stewed beef noodle soup, not unlike the Chili Cook-Offs in the U.S.

Part of the secret to this dish is how the beef is prepared, first boiled then flash-seared in a pot with spices to seal in the flavor. You know the soup is done when you can taste the rich flavor of the beef in the broth.

The assembly of this dish is just as important as the soup itself. First you fill individual bowls with the beef soup stock, add boiled noodles and spinach, and top with pieces of the beef, fresh garlic, cilantro, and drizzled hot pepper oil. This is an "off menu" dish that is loved by our whole family.

Stewed beef

2 lb. pot roast or rump roast beef
4 cloves garlic (peeled)
3 Tbs. rice wine
½ cup soy sauce
½ Tbs. salt
3 Tbs. vegetable oil
2 Tbs. hot pepper oil
7–8 cups water

Beef spice

2 scallion stalks (chopped)
¼ cup ginger root (cubed)
1 Tbs. star anise
5 dried chilli peppers
Spice bag

Noodles & Individual bowl preparation

3-4 oz. flour noodles per bowl (dry or fresh)
Handful spinach per bowl
1 tsp. garlic per bowl (diced fine)
1 Tbs. cilantro per bowl (chopped)
1 Tbs. scallions per bowl (diced fine)
Hot pepper oil (for drizzling)

1. Cut beef into 2-inch cubes.
2. Place scallions, ginger root, star anise and dry chilli peppers into spice bag until ready to use.
3. In a large pot, heat 3 Tbs. vegetable oil over high heat until hot. Add garlic and cook for 1–2 minutes (until aromatic). Add beef cubes, stir and cook until no longer red on the outside, approximately 3–4 minutes.
4. Add rice wine, soy sauce, salt, water and spice bag. Cook on medium heat for 45 minutes.
5. Remove beef from heat. Carefully remove spice bag and discard. Add hot pepper oil and mix together.
6. Add garlic, cilantro, and scallions to large soup bowls. Set aside.
7. Fill a medium pot ¾ full with hot water and bring to a boil. Add noodles and cook until done (approximately 4 minutes) or according to package instructions. Turn off heat, add spinach and mix well. Drain water and divide noodles and spinach across each bowl.
8. Pour beef soup into each bowl, top with cooked beef, a drizzle of hot pepper oil, and serve hot.

Oyster Flavored Beef

(4–6 servings)

This is a classic Cantonese-style dish from the Guangdong province of China, where my father was born. This dish was one of his favorites. When I prepare this dish, I stick to the traditional ingredients and methods. I had to add this recipe to the cookbook, as it has always been a favorite of my students and of my customers. This no-fuss recipe is easy to make and is always a crowd pleaser.

10 oz. beef tenderloin (sliced thin)
2 cloves garlic (crushed)
1 Tbs. ginger root (thinly sliced)
1 red pepper (cubed)
3 cups vegetable oil for frying
2 Tbs. vegetable oil

Marinade

⅛ tsp. baking soda
½ tsp. salt
½ Tbs. arrowroot (can be substituted with cornstarch)
1 Tbs. rice wine
1 Tbs. water

Sauce

3 Tbs. oyster sauce
½ Tbs. soy sauce
½ tsp. honey
1 Tbs. water
½ Tbs. arrowroot (can be substituted with cornstarch)

1. In a bowl, combine marinade ingredients and mix thoroughly. Mix beef with marinade.
2. In a separate bowl, combine sauce ingredients and mix thoroughly. Set aside.
3. Heat 3 cups vegetable oil in a pot over high heat until very hot (350°F). Add beef carefully and fry in oil for one minute, then remove.
4. Heat 2 Tbs. vegetable oil in a wok or large frying pan until hot and add garlic and ginger. Stir-fry over high heat for a few seconds.
5. Add cubed red pepper and continue to stir-fry over high heat for 1 minute.
6. Add beef, sauce and mix well. Remove from heat and serve.

Sichuan-style Stewed Beef with Carrots

(6–8 servings)

In Chinese, we call this method huong chao, which means red stewing. Sichuan-style meat dishes often involve a long marinating time as well as the use of stewing in order to ensure a deep penetration of flavor. Whenever my mother made this for our family, the enticing aroma would permeate the whole house and beyond, and make everyone in the neighborhood hungry like they hadn't eaten for days!

Sichuan dishes are often spicy, and that is how my mother made this dish. In this recipe, I have toned down the heat but kept the aromatic flavors intact. The result is a succulent, tender, and flavorful sliced beef perfectly complemented by the sweetness of the carrots. Your house will be filled with this lovely aroma when you make this dish. It was an instant hit in our classes and after 35 years, it's still an easy favorite.

1½ lbs. beef (pot roast)
2 carrots (peeled)
4 Tbs. vegetable oil
3 cloves garlic (peeled)
1 Tbs. honey
½ cup soy sauce
3 Tbs. rice wine
2 Tbs. hot pepper oil
1 cup water

Spices for beef
1 scallion stalk (chopped)
1 star anise
1 tsp. Chinese brown peppercorn
1 cup ginger root (peeled and cubed)
Spice bag

1. Cut beef and carrots into 1½-inch cubes.
2. Place scallions, star anise, peppercorn, and ginger in a spice bag until ready to use.
3. Heat vegetable oil in a deep pot over high heat until hot. Add garlic and stir for a few seconds to release flavor. Add beef and stir briefly until seared and brown on all sides. Gradually add soy sauce, rice wine, water, honey, and finally the spice bag.
4. Cover pot, reduce heat to medium, and cook for 30–40 minutes.
5. Add carrots and hot pepper oil. Cover and cook for another 20–25 minutes over medium heat or until beef and carrots are tender. Remove from heat and serve.

Jung Bao Beef

(4–6 servings)

Jung bao means "fast cooking" with marinated beef. My first beginner students loved this recipe from the earliest days; they were so surprised at how easy it was to make and how good it tasted. My father told me this recipe originated from the northern province of China. I learned to love this dish growing up in Taiwan, where it was served in many restaurants.

This is an authentic Chinese recipe not commonly found in restaurants in the United States. It is still part of my beginner classes today and is popular in our carry-out.

12 oz. beef sirloin
2 Tbs. soy sauce
1 Tbs. arrowroot (can be substituted with cornstarch)
1 bunch scallions
4 Tbs. vegetable oil

Sauce

2 Tbs. sweet bean sauce (can be substituted with hoisin sauce)
2 Tbs. rice wine
¼ tsp. honey
1 Tbs. sesame oil

1. Slice beef very thin. Combine with soy sauce and arrowroot in a bowl. Set aside.
2. Combine sauce ingredients in a small bowl. Set aside.
3. Clean and cut scallions into 2-inch lengths.
4. Heat 3 Tbs. vegetable oil in a wok or large frying pan until very hot. Add beef and stir-fry for 1–2 minutes or until done. Remove beef from pan.
5. Using the same wok or pan heat 1 Tbs. vegetable oil, add sauce mixture and cook for a few seconds. Add scallions and stir-fry until hot. Return beef back into pan and mix well. Remove from heat and serve.

Ginger Beef with Celery

(4–6 servings)

When I first started teaching Chinese cooking in the Seacoast area in the early 1980s, ginger was available in the local supermarkets, but I didn't see it used much as an ingredient in local restaurants. I decided to write more recipes using ginger because it is such a staple of Chinese cooking, and because of all the health benefits it provides for the human body. This recipe is a wonderful blend of finely shredded ginger, marinated beef, and traditional chinese flavors.

12–14 oz. lean beef (any cut, sliced)
⅓ cup ginger root (shredded)
2½ cups celery (sliced thin)
¼ cup cilantro (chopped)
1 cup vegetable oil (for blanching)

Marinade

2 Tbs. rice wine
1 Tbs. arrowroot (can be substituted with cornstarch)
1 Tbs. vegetable oil
2 Tbs. soy sauce

Sauce

½ Tbs. honey
1 tsp. salt
½ cup chicken soup stock (see Unique Ingredients section)
½ tsp. rice vinegar
1½ Tbs. arrowroot (can be substituted with cornstarch)
1 Tbs. hot pepper oil

1. In a large bowl, combine marinade ingredients and mix with sliced beef. Set aside for 15 minutes.
2. In a separate bowl, mix sauce ingredients and set aside.
3. In a wok or medium pot heat 1 cup vegetable oil on high heat until hot (350°F). Blanch beef in oil until almost done (approximately 45–60 seconds). Do not overcook the beef. Remove from heat. Remove beef from pan and drain oil.
4. Using the same pan coated in oil, add ginger and celery, stir-fry until very hot (approximately 2 minutes). Add sauce and stir until thickened. Mix in beef. Add cilantro and mix well. Remove from heat and serve.

Chicken with Cashews in *Ma La* Sauce

(4–6 servings)

My mother used to make a similar dish for our family. At that time, it was typical for mothers to teach the girls in the household how to cook. My mother believed that this was her duty. I remember her saying to my sisters and me that if we had nothing else to do in life, we would always have food to eat.

People ask me all the time, what is ma la? Early in my career teaching Chinese cooking, a student asked me this question and it sparked the idea to write this recipe. Ma is a spice that has a static and slightly numbing quality on the tongue, while la, means spicy hot. Paired together, they form the unique ingredients of this dish and are a favorite and staple spice mixture in Sichuan cooking. This recipe was an instant hit in my cooking classes. Years later, I decided to add it to our carry-out menu. It's remained such a popular dish that, to this day, some customers will order it every single time they come in.

1 lb. chicken meat (cut into 1-inch cubes)
1½ cup cashews (roasted)
1 cup bamboo shoots (cut in ½-inch cubes)
1 green pepper (cut in ½-inch cubes)
2 Tbs. garlic (chopped)
2 Tbs. ginger root (chopped)
1 Tbs. ground peppercorn
1 cup vegetable oil (for blanching)
3 Tbs. vegetable oil

Marinade
1½ Tbs. rice wine
1½ Tbs. soy sauce
½ tsp salt
1½ Tbs. arrowroot (can be substituted with cornstarch)

Sauce
2 Tbs. soy sauce
1 tsp salt
1 Tbs. honey
½ cup chicken soup stock
1½ Tbs. arrowroot (can be substituted with cornstarch)
1 tsp. rice vinegar
1 Tbs. hot pepper oil

1. In a large bowl, combine marinade ingredients.
2. Mix cubed chicken with marinade and set aside for 15 minutes.
3. In a separate bowl, combine sauce ingredients and mix well.
4. Heat 1 cup vegetable oil on high heat until hot (350°F). Blanch chicken in oil until almost done (approximately 1½ minutes). Remove and drain oil.
5. In a wok or large frying pan, heat 3 Tbs. of vegetable oil over medium/high heat until hot. Add garlic, ginger, peppercorn and cook for 10 seconds.
6. Add bamboo shoots and green pepper, mix well and stir-fry for 2 minutes.
7. Add chicken, cashews, and sauce mix until the mixture thickens. Remove from heat and serve.

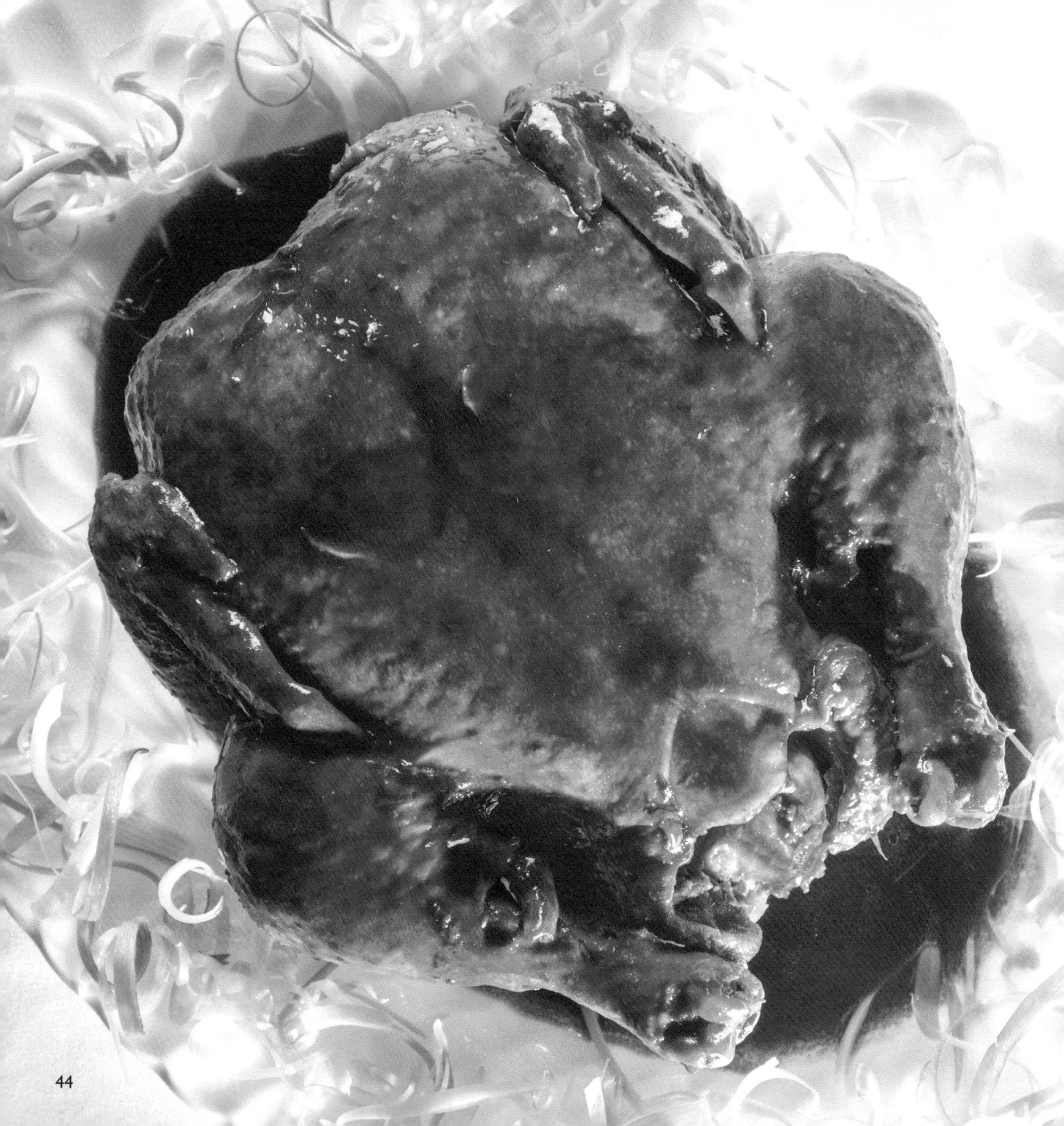

Braised Soy Sauce Chicken

(8–10 servings)

I absolutely adore this recipe. Also known as Soy Sauce Chicken, this is a very popular Cantonese dish. For anyone who has ventured into Chinatown in Boston, New York, or San Francisco, they will have seen these cooked chickens hanging in the window in many restaurants. The beauty of this dish is in its simplicity of preparation. It is always well received by everyone, with its inviting look and tasty flavors. To prepare this dish, the chicken is braised in a complex blend of spices until the juices slowly simmer down into a thick sauce at the bottom of the pan. The chicken is sliced and drizzled with the delicate pan sauce.

3 lbs. whole chicken
½ cup soy sauce
3 Tbs. rice wine
1 Tbs. honey
1 cup water

Chicken spice
1 tsp. star anise
1 tsp. Chinese brown peppercorn
2 scallion stalks
1-inch cinnamon stick
Spice bag

1. Combine star anise, brown peppercorn, scallions and cinnamon stick in a cloth spice bag.
2. Rinse and clean chicken, pat dry with paper towels and set aside.
3. In a deep pot, combine 1 cup of water with the spice bag and bring to boil.
4. Add soy sauce, wine, and honey and cook for a few minutes or until liquid thickens slightly into a sauce and is well blended.
5. Place chicken into the pot with sauce, breast side down and cover.
6. Stew for about 30 minutes over medium heat, turning the chicken every 10 minutes.
7. Remove the chicken and let it set for a few minutes.
8. Collect sauce from the bottom of the pot and stir until mixed well.
9. Slice the chicken into pieces, drizzle with pan sauce, and serve.

Chicken Stir-fried with Broccoli

(4–6 servings)

If I didn't include this dish in my cookbook, I know a lot of our carry-out customers would be disappointed because it has been one of our most popular selections for over 20 years. This is a wonderful Americanized Chinese dish beloved across the U.S. Our version begins with sliced chicken breast perfectly marinated and stir-fried with broccoli in a wonderful light-colored sauce.

12 oz. chicken breast (sliced)
1 ½ cup broccoli (cut into 2-inch lengths and blanched in boiling water for 1 minute)
1 Tbs. scallions (diced)
½ tsp. garlic (finely chopped)
1 Tbs. sesame oil
4 Tbs. vegetable oil

Marinade

1 Tbs. arrowroot (can be substituted with cornstarch)
1 ½ Tbs. soy sauce

Sauce

1 tsp. honey
1 ½ Tbs. soy sauce
½ Tbs. oyster sauce
1 tsp. rice vinegar
½ tsp. salt

Starch mix

½ Tbs. arrowroot (can be substituted with cornstarch)
1 Tbs. water

1. In a small bowl, combine sauce ingredients, mix well and set aside.
2. In a small dish, combine starch mix ingredients until dissolved, and set aside.
3. In a seperate bowl, combine marinade ingredients with chicken and mix thoroughly.
4. In a wok or large frying pan, heat 3 Tbs. vegetable oil on high heat until hot and stir-fry chicken until it is done (approximately 2–3 minutes). Remove chicken from the pan and drain oil.
5. Using the same wok or pan heat 1 Tbs. vegetable oil on high heat until hot and add garlic & scallions. Cook for 10–15 seconds.
6. Add blanched broccoli and mix well. Add sauce and chicken, and stir well until blended and hot. Add starch mix and sesame oil and mix well. Remove from heat and serve.

General Tso's Chicken

(4–6 servings)

General Tso's Chicken has been one of the most popular dishes in our carry-out for years. We receive regular compliments on our adaptation of the dish, so I wanted to pass along our recipe. A little-known fact is that General Tso was an actual general in the Hunan province of China, but this dish was actually created in New York City, after the owner of a Chinese restaurant travelled to Taiwan and tasted a similar dish, which he then improvised for the American palate. At face value, this dish appears to be very simple, but it is actually more complex than people realize. There are two critical components to this dish: double-fried chicken, and a delicate yet complex sauce made with many ingredients to create the right flavor.

We first introduced General Tso's Chicken to our menu in the early 1990s. Each time I tried it in Chinese restaurants in Boston, it tasted a little different, so I set out to write a better version of this dish for our carry-out. The highlight of the dish is the sauce, which is a balancing act of texture and flavor. Our sauce gently coats the chicken while being a little sweet, but not overly sweet, a little tangy but not overly tangy, and a little spicy but not overly spicy.

1 ½ lbs. chicken leg meat cut into 2-inch cubes (may be substituted with breast meat)
2 scallion stalks (cut into 2-inch pieces)
2 Tbs. ginger root (finely chopped)
2 cups broccoli (cut in 2-inch pieces and blanched in boiling water for 1 minute)
4 chilli peppers (dry)
½ Tbs. garlic (diced fine)
1 Tbs. scallion (diced)
½ Tbs. sesame oil
1 tsp. hot pepper oil
1 tsp. salt
4 cups vegetable oil (for frying)
1 Tbs. vegetable oil

Starch mix
1 ½ Tbs. Arrowroot (can be substituted with cornstarch)
3 Tbs. water

Marinade and batter
½ tsp. salt
6 Tbs. arrowroot
1 egg white
2 Tbs. water

Sauce
3 Tbs. sugar
2 Tbs. rice wine
¼ tsp. white pepper
½ Tbs. hoisin sauce
4 Tbs. soy sauce
½ Tbs. dark soy sauce (can be substituted with regular soy sauce)
2 Tbs. rice vinegar
½ Tbs. ketchup
1 Tbs. oyster sauce
½ Tbs. MSG (optional)

Continued on next page...

...continued.

1. In a small bowl, combine sauce ingredients, mix well and set aside.
2. In a separate bowl, combine marinade and batter ingredients, mix well and set aside.
3. In a small dish, combine starch mix ingredients mix until dissolved, and set aside.
4. In a large bowl, rub chicken meat with 1 tsp. salt. Mix in marinade and stir together ensuring chicken is coated well.
5. In in a large pot, heat 4 cups vegetable oil on high heat until hot (350°F) and deep fry chicken until cooked and crispy (approximately 2–3 minutes). Remove chicken from oil and set aside.
6. In a wok or large frying pan, heat ½ Tbs. vegetable oil, cook scallion stalks and ginger for a few seconds until aromatic. Mix in sauce and stir well until hot. Turn off heat and set sauce aside in a small bowl.
7. Reheat oil (375°F) and refry chicken a second time until crispy (approximately 2 minutes).
8. In the wok or large frying pan, heat ½ Tbs. vegetable oil on high heat until hot. Add hot peppers, diced scallions, and garlic and cook for a few seconds. Add sauce, broccoli, chicken, hot pepper oil, sesame oil, and starch mix to thicken. Mix well, remove from heat, and serve.

General Tso's Chicken in North Hampton, 1995

Beijing Roast Duck

(8–10 servings)

I always knew 'Beijing Duck' to be called 'Beiping Duck'. Beiping (meaning 'Northern Peace') is the old name for the city of Beijing, which means 'Northern Capital'. This is the official dish of China, and considered one of the most delicious dishes in Chinese cuisine. While this is a more advanced recipe, I have successfully taught my students how to make it at home by following each step carefully. I decided to include this recipe in my cookbook because it's such an important dish in China, and I want those that love this dish to know that it can be made at home.

Duck is typically a very fatty poultry, but in this preparation, much of the fat is separated from the duck when it is cooked. Done properly, the result is a perfectly browned and crisp skin.

Beijing Duck is typically served thinly sliced, accompanied with a traditional sauce, and wrapped in a homemade flour pancake.

4–5 lb. whole duck
2 scallion bunches (washed and sliced 2½ inches long)

Syrup
3 Tbs. honey
2 Tbs. rice wine
1 Tbs. rice vinegar

Sauce
3 Tbs. sweet bean paste
1 Tbs. sesame oil
1 Tbs. honey
¼ cup water

Thin pancakes
3 cups flour
1 cup boiling water
1 Tbs. vegetable oil

Equipment
1 small steel skewer with loop at one end
Cooking twine
Drinking straw
Cooking brush

Preparing the duck:

1. 7–10 hours before cooking: Rinse duck clean and pat dry with paper towels. Using the small skewer and twine, sew the neck and body cavity of the duck tightly closed except for a small hole for the straw. Be sure there are no air leaks. Insert the tip of the straw into the cavity of the duck and blow to inflate the duck as much as possible. Remove the straw and seal the hole with the skewer and twine.

2. In a small bowl, combine syrup ingredients and mix well.

3. Brush syrup mix all over the outside skin of the duck. Hang the duck in an open space to dry. After 2 hours, coat the duck a second time with syrup. Let the duck dry for a minimum of 5 hours. (Drying the duck in front of a fan in a cool room or placing on a rack in the refrigerator for 48 hours is ideal).

Continued on next page...

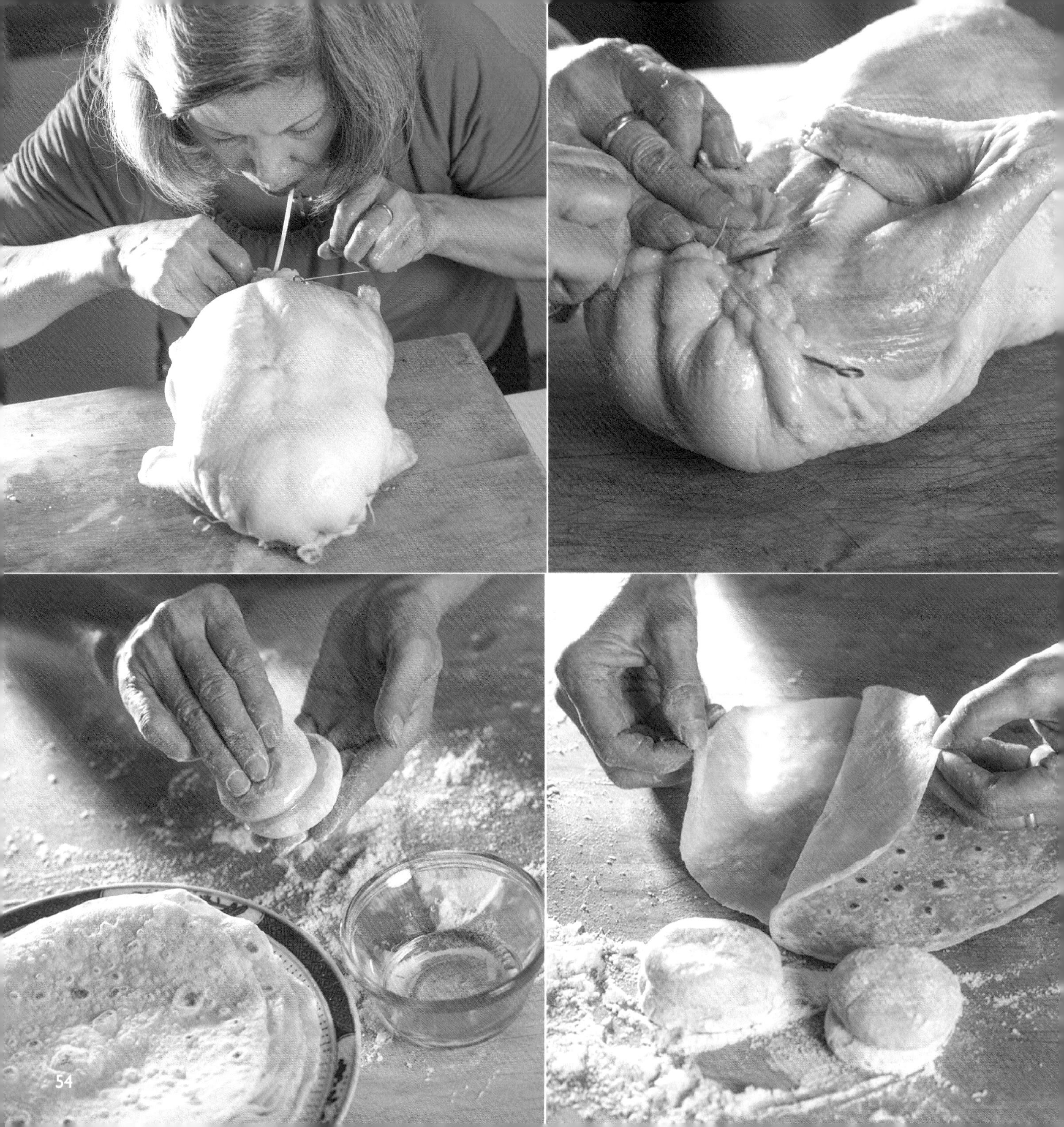

Making thin pancakes:

4. Pour boiling water slowly onto flour in a bowl and mix with wooden spoon. Use caution to avoid burning yourself. Knead the dough with your hands until it is very smooth with no lumps. Cover the dough with plastic and let it rest for 15 minutes.

5. Place dough on lightly floured board or clean counter top. Divide dough into 2 halves. Roll each half of the dough into a long tube (approximately 15 inches long by 2 inches thick). Cut each tube into 12–14 pieces 1½ inches in size. Using a rolling pin or palm of your hand, flatten each piece into a small round thin pancake. Lightly coat the top of each pancake dough with vegetable oil. Lay a second flattened pancake on top of oiled side of previous pancake (stacked on top of each other). Using the rolling pin or your palm, pat down the stack until the pancakes are very thin (approximately 5 inches in diameter).

6. In an ungreased frying pan, heat 2 stacked pancakes at a time on medium-low heat for approximately 1 minute or until bubbles form under the dough and begin to rise. Turn over the pancake and cook the other side for an additional minute.

7. Remove pancake from heat, cover with a damp cloth for 10 seconds, then separate the 2 pancakes by slowly pulling apart.

8. Cook the remaining pancakes in the same way. Store pancakes under damp cloth or sealed in a bag until ready to eat.

Roasting the duck:

9. Heat oven to 375°F and cook duck for 30 minutes, breast side up, on a roasting rack and pan. Turn heat down to 275°F and cook for an additional 30 minutes or until meat is done. Duck should be nicely browned on the outside. Remove from oven and set aside to cool.

10. In a small pan, combine sauce ingredients and bring to a slow boil over medium heat, stirring until thickened. Remove from heat and pour into a small serving dish.

11. After the duck has cooled, carve by first slicing the skin off duck and then the meat into thin slices. Arrange meat in center of serving platter with skin arranged around outside edge.

How to eat:

Take one piece each of duck meat, crispy skin, and scallion, place them in the center of a pancake, then brush with sauce. Roll up and enjoy!

Minced Cornish Game Hens

(4–6 servings)

When I was still teaching out of my home kitchen in Rye, a friend of the family who was an Air Force pilot asked about a delicious dish called Minced Pigeon, a delicacy in Shanghai, that he had tried and loved during his posting in Asia. I told him I would make it for him the next time he came to visit.

At that time, I was still learning about the American palate. When I went to our meat market to ask if they carried pigeon, the butcher looked at me cross-eyed. I knew right then, something was not right. Pigeon was not part of the traditional western diet. I still wanted to make this dish, so I began researching other poultry that might be a suitable substitute. I learned about an interesting bird called Cornish game hen, and it appeared to be very similar. So I set out to write this recipe using Cornish game hen. When our friend finally came to visit, he gave his seal of approval for the dish, and that finalized it for my cooking classes.

I love this dish because it's unique, healthy, and delicious. This recipe combines Cornish game hen with pork to round out the flavor, with shiitake mushrooms and water chestnuts to add texture, all diced into a fine mince and quickly stir fried in a savory sauce. I serve it in iceberg lettuce cups. It's so fun to eat!

1 lb. Cornish game hen meat (about 2 hens)
3 dried shiitake mushrooms (fresh mushrooms may be used)
4 oz. ground pork
1 Tbs. arrowroot
2 Tbs. soy sauce
1 small onion (diced)
1 Tbs. ginger root (finely chopped)
1 can water chestnuts (rinsed and diced)
1 Tbs. rice wine
1 tsp. salt
1 ½ tsp. honey
1 head of iceberg lettuce
5 Tbs. vegetable oil

1. Soak mushrooms (if dried) in warm water until softened, then dice.
2. Rinse each hen clean with water and remove skin. Remove meat from bones and mince.
3. Peel off each lettuce leaf, and wash leaves well.
4. In a large bowl, combine diced hen, ground pork, arrowroot, and soy sauce and mix well.
5. In a wok or large frying pan, heat vegetable oil over high heat. Stir-fry diced onion for a few seconds, then add ginger, mushrooms, and water chestnuts and stir-fry for another few seconds.
6. Add meat and stir-fry over high heat until all ingredients are well mixed together and meat is cooked thoroughly (approximately 2–3 minutes). Add rice wine, salt and honey. Mix well until hot, and remove from heat.
7. Place mixture on top of 3 large lettuce leaves arranged like a bowl.
8. To serve, take 1 large leaf of lettuce, fill with cooked mixture, fold like a taco, and enjoy!

Honey Cornish Game Hen with Vegetables

(4–6 servings)

In the Seacoast area of New England in the early 1980s, cooking with Cornish game hens was rare. When I did see it on the menu in restaurants, it was typically baked or roasted. Most homes in Taiwan didn't have an oven when I was growing up, so our food was usually steamed, stir-fried, or deep fried. I thought it would be interesting to try cooking a Cornish game hen using more traditional Chinese cooking methods, so I wrote this recipe to give my students a different perspective of how this western poultry could be prepared.

1 lb. Cornish hen meat (about 2 hens, cut in large slices)
1 cup celery (sliced)
1 cup red peppers (sliced)
2 scallion stalks (sliced thin)
2 Tbs. sesame oil
1 cup vegetable oil (for blanching)
3 Tbs. vegetable oil

Marinade

2 Tbs. light soy sauce
1 Tbs. rice wine
1½ Tbs. arrowroot (can be substituted with cornstarch)
1 Tbs. vegetable oil
1 Tbs. garlic (minced)

Sauce

3 Tbs. light soy sauce
2 Tbs. honey (or syrup)
1½ tsp. vinegar
1 cup chicken soup stock (beef stock can be substituted)
1 Tbs. ginger root (grated)
1 Tbs. rice wine
1½ Tbs. arrowroot (can be substituted with cornstarch)
1 Tbs. sugar

1. Combine marinade ingredients, mix well.
2. In a large bowl, mix sliced Cornish game hen with marinade, set aside for 15–30 minutes.
3. In a separate bowl, combine sauce ingredients, mix well and set aside.
4. In a wok or large frying pan, heat 1 cup vegetable oil over high heat until hot and blanch Cornish game hen meat until cooked. Remove from pan and drain oil.
5. In the same wok or frying pan, heat 3 Tbs. vegetable oil over high heat until hot. Add celery, red peppers, and scallion and stir-fry for 1 minute or until sizzling and hot. Add sauce and cook until thickened.
6. Add cooked meat and sesame oil in pan with vegetables and mix well. Remove from heat and serve.

Pearl Balls

(Approximately 25–30 pieces)

I learned how to make pearl balls when I was in elementary school. My mother played a regular game of Mahjong with a few women in our neighborhood. They would take turns hosting the game each week, and each of the guests would bring a dish so the host wouldn't have to cook. One night, when my mother was hosting, a guest brought seasoned pork meatballs from her home province that were completely covered in sticky rice, so they resembled large pearls. I had never seen anything like it before and the first time I tried it, I immediately fell in love. They are a no fuss, easy-to-make main dish or even an appetizer.

1 cup glutinous rice
2 Tbs. scallion (chopped)
1 lb. ground pork
1 tsp. ginger root (chopped fine)
1 Tbs. soy sauce
½ tsp. salt
1 egg
2 Tbs. arrowroot (can be substituted with cornstarch)
Thin cloth or iceberg lettuce (for steaming)

1. Soak glutinous rice in cold water for approximately 30 minutes and drain.
2. In a large bowl, mix the scallions, ginger, soy sauce, salt, egg, 1 Tbs. arrowroot, and pork. Stir together until the mixture becomes very thick.
3. Sprinkle 1 Tbs. arrowroot across a large tray and put glutinous rice on top.
4. Wet one hand. Place a portion of the pork mixture in palm of hand and close fingers to roll and form a meatball the size of a large walnut (approximately 2–3 Tbs.).
5. Put all the meatballs on top of the glutinous rice in the tray and shake the tray back and forth until glutinous rice sticks to all sides of the meatballs (roll around as necessary to cover all sides with rice).
6. Place meatballs in a steamer on a damp cloth or large pieces of iceberg lettuce so they do not stick to the bottom and steam 20 to 30 minutes over high heat.
7. Remove and serve while hot.

Sichuan-style Pork with Garlic Sauce

(4–6 servings)

My mother had the greatest influence in my culinary training, and in shaping my perspective on food. Sichuan-style pork with garlic sauce was her personal favorite. To make this dish, my mother would boil pork until it was nice and tender, then slice it thin. What makes this dish absolutely stand out is the sauce, a flavorful blend of chopped fresh garlic, soy sauce, and sesame paste, combined with hot pepper oil that adds a rich deep red color, and a touch of honey to add a slight sweetness.

I included this recipe in my classes to commemorate my mother and her memory. This was a dish reserved for my more advanced classes, because it has a level of spiciness that isn't always for the beginner palate.

1 lb. pork loin
2 scallion stalks (diced)

Sauce

1½ Tbs. garlic (minced)
4 Tbs. soy sauce
2 tsp. honey
1 Tbs. sesame paste
1 Tbs. sesame oil
1 Tbs. hot pepper oil
⅛ tsp. MSG (optional)

1. Place pork in a large pot on stove. Cover with water and bring water to a boil. Reduce heat to medium and cook pork until done, approximately 15 minutes after water is boiling. Remove pork from water and set aside for a few minutes to cool.
2. In a small bowl, combine sauce ingredients and mix well.
3. Using a sharp knife, slice pork very thin and place slices on serving platter.
4. Sprinkle scallions on top and pour sauce on top of scallions and sliced pork.
5. Serve warm or at room temperature.

Goon Bao (Kung Pao) Shrimp

(4–6 servings)

Most people recognize this dish as Kung Pao, but it was taught to me as Goon Bao (in the Sichuan dialect) by my mother, who told me this dish was originally created by a palace chef in the Sichuan province, in honor of the governor. The governor's title was Goon Bao, meaning 'Palace Guardian', and this became known as the palace treasure dish because it was so widely loved.

I use shrimp in our Goon Bao recipe instead of chicken, because that was how it was originally taught to me; however, chicken can easily be substituted. I included this family recipe in my classes because my mother's Goon Bao sauce had such wonderful flavor. It is a little sweet from honey, slightly tangy from rice wine, with a hint of spiciness from red chilli pepper. Correctly done, the shrimp is marinated in a way that ensures it stays moist and juicy with the right texture and flavor in each bite.

1 lb. medium shrimp (peeled and deveined)
1 cup celery (diced)
1 cup roasted peanuts
8–10 chilli peppers (dry)
1 Tbs. garlic (diced)
3 Tbs. scallion (diced)
1 Tbs. rice wine
1 cup vegetable oil (for frying)
3 Tbs. vegetable oil

Marinade

1 Tbs. arrowroot (can be substituted with cornstarch)
2 tsp. grated ginger root
1 Tbs. soy sauce

Sauce

3 Tbs. soy sauce
½ tsp salt
1½ Tbs. honey
1 Tbs. arrowroot (can be substituted with cornstarch)
1 Tbs. sesame oil
1½ Tbs. rice wine
4 Tbs. chicken soup stock (see Unique ingredients section)

1. In a small bowl, combine marinade ingredients, mix well and set aside.
2. In a separate small bowl, combine sauce ingredients, mix well and set aside.
3. Rinse shrimp clean with cold water and pat dry with paper towel.
4. In a large bowl, combine shrimp with rice wine and mix well. Add marinade to the shrimp, mix thoroughly and set aside.
5. In a wok or large frying pan, heat 1 cup vegetable oil over medium-high heat until hot (350°F). Add dried chilli pepper and cook for a couple seconds until dark in color. Add shrimp and mix until shrimp is cooked through (approximately 1½ minutes). Remove from pan or wok and drain oil.
6. In the same pan or wok, heat 3 Tbs. vegetable oil over high heat, add garlic, celery, and sauce and mix well. Cook until sauce has slightly thickened.
7. Add peanuts, shrimp and scallions and mix to combine. Remove from heat and serve.

Prawns with Tomato Sauce

(4–6 servings)

When I first came to New England in the mid-70s, the Seacoast area reminded me of the east coast of China, where seafood is also a staple of the local diet. This recipe brings back fond memories of a wonderful dish that I loved in China. To keep it tender and juicy, the shrimp is first cooked in its shell, where it retains its moisture and absorbs the flavor. What is most appealing about this dish is how gorgeous and enticing it looks, with the deep red color accented by fresh green scallions. It's so simple to make, yet elegant; a fantastic option when you want to impress company in your home, or make something special for your family.

1 lb. jumbo prawns (in their shells)
1 tsp. salt
1 cup chicken soup stock or water (see Unique Ingredients section)
1 Tbs. ginger root (diced)
1 Tbs. arrowroot (can be substituted with cornstarch)
5 Tbs. vegetable oil
1 Tbs. rice wine
1 tsp. honey
2 scallion stalks (2-inch lengths)
4 Tbs. tomato ketchup
2 Tbs. water

Starch mix

1 ½ Tbs. arrowroot (can be substituted with cornstarch)
3 Tbs. water

1. Retain shell, and cut each shrimp along the back with a paring knife and devein. Trim off tail and legs. Rinse clean with cold water and pat dry with paper towels.
2. In a large bowl, combine shrimp with arrowroot and water and mix thoroughly. Set aside.
3. Combine starch mix ingredients until dissolved, and set aside.
4. In a large wok or frying pan, heat 4 Tbs. vegetable oil over high heat. Stir-fry the shrimp until both sides turn red. Add rice wine, salt, honey and soup stock. Cook for about 3 minutes. Remove from pan and set aside.
5. In the same wok or frying pan, heat 1 Tbs. vegetable oil over high heat, stir-fry ginger root and scallions for a few seconds then add tomato ketchup. Cook for a few seconds and return shrimp mixture to pan and cook together for approximately 1 minute. Add starch mix, stir until thickened. Remove from heat and serve.

Popped Rice Shrimp Fantasy

(4–6 servings)

This is one of the most unique dishes in this cookbook. Once you observe how it's made or try it yourself, you will appreciate how amazing it is. The original concept for this recipe came from a very clever chef in China who was experimenting with burnt rice at the bottom of his rice cooker. Usually this was scraped off and thrown away, but this chef decided to try something different with it. He dried the brown crispy rice and placed it in hot oil. The result was light popped rice, similar to popcorn, that soaked up the flavor from any sauce poured on it.

This dish begins with a pan coated with a bed of popped rice. Then a blend of shrimp, chicken, mushrooms, and sugar snap peas is stir-fried in a light sauce and poured over the top. The result is a satisfying sizzle as the dish is served and the rice absorbs the wonderful flavor of the sauce.

8 oz. shrimp (peeled and deveined)
2 oz. chicken breast (sliced)
2 oz. cooked ham (cut in 2-inch slices)
6 pcs. dried shiitake mushrooms (fresh mushrooms may be used)
2 oz. sugar snap peas
3 oz. bamboo shoots (sliced thin)
1 scallion stalk (cut into long thin strips)
1½ cups chicken soup stock (see Unique Ingredients section)
1 Tbs. soy sauce
2 Tbs. arrowroot (can be substituted with cornstarch)
½ tsp. salt
2½ cups vegetable oil (for popping rice)
3 Tbs. vegetable oil
1 cup dried crispy rice (see explanation below)

Seasoning for Shrimp & Chicken

1 tsp. arrowroot (can be substituted with cornstarch)
¼ tsp. salt
1/8 tsp. baking soda

Dried crispy rice (prepared 2-3 days in advance)

1–2 cups pre-cooked rice in a rice cooker or on the stove
Large baking tray

Continued on next page...

...continued.

1. 2–3 days in advance of preparing this dish, spread out cooked rice across a large baking pan and set out in room temperature for a couple days to dry. The rice is done when it has become very hard and slightly translucent.
2. When ready to prepare the dish, begin by soaking mushrooms in warm water (if dried) until soft. Cut off stems and discard.
3. Rinse shrimp with cold water and pat dry with paper towels.
4. In a large bowl, combine shrimp, chicken with seasoning ingredients and mix thoroughly.
5. In a small bowl, mix ½ cup soup stock with arrowroot until dissolved to make arrowroot mix.
6. In a wok or large frying pan, heat 3 Tbs. vegetable oil over high heat. Add shrimp and chicken and saute until shrimp is red and chicken is cooked, approximately 2 minutes. Remove shrimp and chicken from pan.
7. In the same wok or pan, boil remaining soup stock with mushrooms for a few minutes. Add bamboo shoots, sugar snap peas, ham, salt, and soy sauce. Reduce heat to low and add shrimp and chicken. Slowly stir in arrowroot mix. Add scallions and continue to stir until thickened.
8. In a clean wok or deep frying pan, heat remaining vegetable oil until very hot (375°F). Fry dried crispy rice (rice should "pop" within 3 seconds) for a few seconds, strain popped rice and drain excess oil. Spread crispy rice on warmed serving platter.
9. Quickly pour shrimp mix over rice and serve immediately.

Heavenly Seafood Delight

(4–6 servings)

I set out to create a dish that brought together all of New England's best seafood. When I wrote this recipe, I originally called it Seafood Delight because it was a delightful combination of scallops, shrimp, and lobster. I immediately fell in love with this recipe after I wrote it, not only for the wonderful blend of flavors, but also for the beautiful, colorful look of the dish. To this day, it is one of the most popular dishes from our catering menu.

One of my first students was an 85-year-old young man. He was always an active participant in class and a very inquisitive learner. He also happened to be a connoisseur of good vodka, which usually meant he came to class with an outgoing, jovial personality. I will never forget that, when he tried this dish for the first time, he exclaimed loudly, "This isn't Seafood Delight, this is Heavenly Seafood Delight!" Everyone around the table laughed, but the name stuck. I decided to change it in honor of this student who loved this dish.

Continued on next page...

...continued.

½ lb. medium size shrimp (peeled and deveined)
½ lb. lobster meat (cooked and sliced)
½ lb. scallops (sliced)
1 can straw mushrooms
½ lb. bok choy (sliced)
1 Tbs. garlic (minced)
1 Tbs. ginger root (minced)
1 tsp. salt
5 Tbs. vegetable oil

Marinade
1 Tbs. rice wine
1 Tbs. arrowroot (can be substituted with cornstarch)
½ tsp. salt
2 Tbs. vegetable oil

Sauce
3 Tbs. oyster sauce
2 Tbs. soy sauce
1 Tbs. hot pepper oil
1½ Tbs. arrowroot (can be substituted with cornstarch)
½ cup chicken soup stock

1. Rinse shrimp clean with cold water and pat dry with paper towel.
2. In a large bowl, combine marinade ingredients, mix well until dissolved. Add shrimp, scallops, and lobster. Set aside.
3. In a small bowl, combine sauce ingredients, mix well until dissolved and set aside.
4. In the pan or wok, heat 3 Tbs. vegetable oil over high heat until hot. Stir-fry garlic and ginger for a few seconds until fragrant. Add shrimp, lobster, and scallops. Cook until shrimp turns red. Remove from pan and set into a dish.
5. In the pan or wok, heat 2 Tbs. vegetable oil over high heat until hot. Add bok choy and mushrooms, cook until hot. Mix in the sauce and cook until thickened. Then add seafood back into pan. Remove from heat and serve.

Scallops Surrounded with Pine Nuts

(4–6 servings)

The idea for this recipe came to me when I was at a local supermarket in Portsmouth. I remember seeing zucchini for the first time and being curious about it because it was not used in any of the Chinese cooking that I was taught. I decided to experiment a bit and combine this vegetable with another more western ingredient, pine nuts, adding a Chinese flair to it. I used New England scallops in this dish because they are so unique, large, beautiful, and fresh from our Seacoast. I practiced different flavors until I perfected this recipe. It became such a hit that a local seafood store asked if they could include the recipe on the side of their scallop packaging. In this rendition, the scallops are marinated ahead of time to give them a rich complex flavor, the pine nuts are flash-fried so they are crispy, and everything is stir-fried together in a pan with zucchini.

1½ lb. of scallops
1 lb. zucchini (cut into long thin slices)
2 scallion stalks (chopped)
¼ cup cilantro (chopped)
½–¾ cup pine nuts
½ tsp. sea salt (can be substituted with regular salt)
4 Tbs. vegetable oil

Marinade

1 Tbs. ginger (grated)
1 Tbs. rice wine
½ tsp. sea salt (can be substituted with regular salt)
½ tsp. white pepper

Sauce

½ cup chicken soup stock (see Unique Ingredients section)
2 Tbs. oyster sauce
1½ Tbs. arrowroot (can be substituted with cornstarch)
½ tsp. white pepper

1. Combine marinade ingredients and mix well.
2. Rinse scallops, pat dry with paper towel. In a large bowl, combine scallops with marinade, mix well and set aside for 15–30 minutes.
3. In a small bowl, combine sauce ingredients, mix well until dissolved and set aside.
4. In a wok or large frying pan, heat 3 Tbs. vegetable oil over high heat until hot. Add pine nuts and stir-fry for 30–45 seconds. Remove nuts from pan and set aside in a bowl. Leave oil in wok and stir-fry scallops until firm or fully cooked, approximately 2–3 minutes. Remove from pan.
5. Heat 1 Tbs. vegetable oil in the same wok or pan over high heat until hot. Add zucchini and salt, and stir-fry until lightly softened, approximately 1–2 minutes. Add scallops and sauce and mix well. Add scallions, cilantro, pine nuts, mix well. Remove from heat and serve.

Brown Sauce Fish

(4–6 servings)

Expect your whole house to smell amazing when you make this dish. In Chinese culture, fish symbolizes prosperity, so it is common to serve this dish when you have guests visit your home. It is also common in Chinese cooking to prepare and serve the entire fish, from head to tail. The head represents the beginning of life, and the end is the completion. Growing up in Taiwan, my mother would always make this when guests came to visit. The harmony of the sweet and spicy sauce permeates the fish while cooking in the pan, and the result is a wonderful layering of complex flavors.

I adapted this dish for a more western palate, using a deboned fillet, to simplify the preparation and make it easier to eat. Otherwise, this recipe is unchanged from its original form. Nearly every student who has learned this recipe from me raves about it.

1½ lbs. fish filet (any whitefish)
¼ cup arrowroot (can be substituted with cornstarch)
½ Tbs. salt
2 cloves garlic (diced)
3 pcs. hot chilli pepper (dried)
1 Tbs. ginger root (grated)
3 Tbs. rice wine
1 Tbs. honey
2½ Tbs. soy sauce
5 Tbs. vegetable oil
½ cup water
3 scallion stalks (cut into long thin strips)
⅛ tsp. MSG (optional)

1. Sprinkle salt evenly on both sides of fish and set aside for a few minutes. Spread a thin layer of arrowroot on waxed paper. Coat fish on both sides.

2. In a large frying pan, heat 4 Tbs. vegetable oil over high heat until hot. Turn heat down and lightly fry fish over medium heat until firm throughout. Remove fish from pan.

3. In a clean frying pan, heat 1 Tbs. vegetable oil. Stir-fry garlic, then add hot chilli pepper until brown. Turn heat low, and add fish, ginger root, rice wine, honey, soy sauce, MSG (if using), and water. Cook for 5 minutes and add scallions on top to finish. Remove from heat and serve.

Ham and Shrimp Fried Rice

(4–6 servings)

In Chinese, we call this 'Yangzhou chao fan', a well-known dish from the Jiangsu province. This is a very simple recipe, and always a great complement to any other dish on your table. Most of the fried rice you find in the U.S. is a dark brown color, because it has been stir fried with soy sauce. This eastern-style fried rice remains white and features a rainbow of colors; rich yellow from scrambled egg, deep red from shrimp, bright green peas, and warm pink from cubed ham. Ham and shrimp are traditionally not served together in western cooking, but this is very popular in Taiwan. You could call it Land and Sea Fried Rice! Chicken, beef, or vegetables can easily be substituted for the shrimp or ham in this very versatile dish.

1 cup medium sized shrimp (peeled and deveined)
½ cup cooked ham (diced)
½ cup green peas (frozen)
2 Tbs. scallion (diced)
2 tsp. rice wine
2 eggs (beaten)
1 pinch baking soda
1 tsp. salt
6 Tbs. vegetable oil
5 cups pre-cooked rice

1. Rinse shrimp clean with cold water and pat dry with paper towel.
2. In a large bowl, combine shrimp with wine and baking soda. Mix well and set aside.
3. In a wok or large frying pan, heat 2 Tbs. oil over medium-high heat until hot and scramble eggs, then remove eggs from wok.
4. In the same wok or frying pan, heat 2 Tbs. vegetable oil over high heat and saute shrimp for 1 minute. Add ham and green peas. Stir and cook for 2 minutes and remove from heat.
5. In the same wok or frying pan, heat 2 Tbs. vegetable oil until hot, then reduce heat to medium and stir-fry cooked rice for 2–3 minutes. Add salt and mix well.
6. Stir egg, shrimp, and ham mixture into rice. Add scallion just before removing from heat and stir well. Serve warm.

Taiwanese-style Stir-fried Rice Noodles

(4–6 servings)

This is the best example of Taiwanese "comfort food". I was introduced to this stir-fried rice noodle as a young teenager and I remember thinking the taste and texture was so different from traditional Chinese flour noodles. I ate so much of this growing up, that I had to include it in this cookbook as a tribute to the local cuisine from my home country. I hope you will enjoy eating this as much as I do.

8–10 oz. package of rice sticks (dried rice noodles)
4 oz. pork loin (cut into thin strips)
4 oz. small shrimp (peeled and deveined)
5–6 shiitake mushrooms (sliced)
½ lb. bean sprouts
1 cup garlic chives (cut into 1-inch pieces) (optional)
½ cup chicken soup stock (see Unique Ingredients section)
4 Tbs. vegetable oil

Marinade
½ Tbs. rice wine
½ Tbs. arrowroot (can be substituted with cornstarch)
½ tsp. salt

Seasoning
1 tsp. white pepper
1 tsp. honey
1 Tbs. sesame oil
3 Tbs. soy sauce
1 tsp. salt

1. Soak rice sticks in very hot water until softened (around 30 minutes). Drain water and cut into 4–5-inch pieces.
2. Rinse shrimp clean with cold water and pat dry with paper towel. Sprinkle with salt. Set aside.
3. Rinse bean sprouts until clean.
4. In a medium sized bowl, combine marinade ingredients until dissolved. Add pork to bowl, mix well, and set aside.
5. In a separate bowl, combine seasoning ingredients, mix well and set aside.
6. In a wok or large frying pan, heat 2 Tbs. vegetable oil over high heat. Stir fry mushrooms for one minute.
7. Turn heat to medium, add shrimp and pork and stir-fry until cooked, approximately 2-3 minutes. Remove from pan and set aside.
8. In the same wok or frying pan, heat 2 Tbs. vegetable oil over high heat. Add garlic chives and bean sprouts and cook for 15–30 seconds. Add soup stock, seasoning, and rice noodles. Continue to stir fry until liquid is evenly absorbed, then mix mushrooms, pork, and shrimp back in. Stir well, remove from heat and serve.

Sichuan Spicy Cold Noodles

(6–10 samll servings)

When I was a little girl growing up in Taiwan, I remember a bicycle vendor in our town who sold homemade cold noodles during the summer. Attached to the back of the bike he had a large bucket of cold noodles, and on the side he carried a mix of sauces and fresh ingredients. He was well known in our town for riding his bike while yelling "Cold Noodles! Cold noodles!" Whenever we heard him pass by, my mother would tell me to flag him down for an afternoon snack. We would hand him an empty bowl, and he would fill it with noodles. On top, he would pour a secret sauce and toss it with fresh garlic, sesame oil and hot pepper oil. Oh my goodness, it was so delicious! I would become so hungry just watching him prepare it for us. When I came to the U.S., I decided to recreate this incredible dish and package it for sale at local markets in the Seacoast area. This dish is simple to make, and pleasant to eat on a hot summer day.

½ lb. lo mein noodles
½ lb. bean sprouts
1 Tbs. vegetable oil

Sauce:
1 Tbs. garlic (finely chopped)
2 Tbs. sesame paste
½ Tbs. sesame oil
1 Tbs. peanut butter
4 Tbs. soy sauce
1 Tbs. honey
2 Tbs. hot pepper oil
½ tsp. MSG (optional)

1. Fill a medium pot ¾ full with hot water and bring to a boil. Blanch bean sprouts for 10 seconds then remove from the pot and rinse with cold water.
2. Cook the lo mein noodles in the boiling water until done (approximately 4 minutes) or according to package instructions. Do not overcook the noodles or allow them to become too soft.
3. Remove noodles from the pot, rinse with cold water and mix with 1 Tbs. vegetable oil to prevent the cooked noodles from sticking together. Set noodles aside.
4. In a bowl, combine sauce ingredients and mix well.
5. In a large serving bowl, combine noodles, bean sprouts, and sauce. Mix well and serve.

Optional: divide noodles and sprouts into 6–10 servings, add sauce on top, and serve individually.

Ma Po Tofu

(4–6 servings)

The story of the origins of this dish, as told to me by my mother, is almost as great as the dish itself. During my mother's childhood in the Sichuan province, there lived an old woman named Ma Po. She was called Ma Po, or "woman with marked face", because she had suffered from an illness that left her face marked with blemishes. Ma Po was famous across the entire province for her tofu, which she sold out of a small street cart. Her unique recipe included stir-fried tofu with fresh garlic, scallions, brown peppercorns, and hot pepper oil. The aroma of the dish would permeate through the entire street, drawing long lines of people.

The dish was originally vegetarian, but if people wanted a meat dish, they would bring Ma Po some ground pork, which she would dice up and mix in the dish. Today, our Ma Po Tofu adheres to the original recipe taught to me by my mother. It has been one of the most popular dishes in both my cooking classes and carry-out.

1 lb. soft or silken tofu
4 oz. ground pork
2 clove garlic (minced)
½ tsp. ginger root (minced)
3 Tbs. scallions (diced)
1 tsp. honey
¼ cup chicken soup stock (see Unique Ingredients section)
1 Tbs. hot bean paste (chili paste)
1 tsp. Chinese brown peppercorns
1 Tbs. sesame oil
3 Tbs. soy sauce
3 Tbs. vegetable oil
½ Tbs. hot pepper oil

Starch mix

½ Tbs. arrowroot (can be substituted with cornstarch)
2 Tbs. water

1. Cut up tofu into 1-inch cubes.
2. Combine starch mix ingredients until dissolved, and set aside.
3. In a wok or large frying pan, heat vegetable oil over high heat until hot. Add garlic and ground pork. Turn heat to medium-high and stir-fry for a few seconds or until fragrant. Add soup stock, soy sauce, ginger root, brown peppercorns, and tofu. Cook for 3–4 minutes.
4. Add hot bean paste and honey, stirring gently and frequently.
5. Add starch mix to pan along with scallions, sesame oil, and hot pepper oil. Mix well, remove from heat and serve.

Sweet and Sour Hot Cabbage

(4–6 servings)

Cabbage is very popular in western cooking, found usually in salads or served as a steamed vegetable. I wanted to showcase the Chinese technique of stir-fry with cabbage. This dish is a harmony of stir-fried cabbage, soy sauce, brown peppercorns, chilli, and honey. This is a very versatile dish and can be served both hot and cold. This dish is so easy to make, and so enjoyable.

2 lb. cabbage
6 pcs. hot chilli peppers (dried)
1 tsp. Chinese brown peppercorns
4 Tbs. vegetable oil
2 Tbs. rice vinegar
1 ½ tsp. salt
3 Tbs. soy sauce
1 Tbs. honey
½ Tbs. sesame oil

1. Clean cabbage and cut into wedges, about 2 inches by 2 inches.

2. In a wok or large frying pan, heat vegetable oil and stir-fry dried hot chilli peppers for a few seconds until they are are dark in color.

3. Add peppercorns and cabbage, turn heat down to medium and cook for approximately 3 minutes, stirring often until cabbage turns soft.

4. Add rice vinegar, salt, soy sauce, honey and sesame oil. Mix together well, remove from heat and serve.

Optional: Can be thickened with 1 Tbs. arrowroot (or cornstarch) pre dissolved in a small dish with ½ Tbs. water.

String Beans with Garlic Sauce

(4–6 servings)

I included this dish because of how popular it is in our carry-out. It's a healthy vegetarian dish that doesn't sacrifice anything in the way of flavor. The string beans are flash fried until they are nice and crunchy, then coated in a brown sauce that is slightly sweet and tangy with a hint of spice. This dish is usually served as a complement to a main dish on the table.

1½ lb. string beans
1½ Tbs. garlic (minced)
½ Tbs. ginger root (chopped)
1 cup vegetable oil (for stir-frying)
2 Tbs. vegetable oil

Sauce
1½ Tbs. honey
½ Tbs. hot pepper oil
1 Tbs. rice wine
2 Tbs. soy sauce
1 tsp. rice vinegar
1 Tbs. sesame oil
½ Tbs. arrowroot (can be substituted with cornstarch)

1. Using your fingers or a small paring knife, remove the ends of the string beans on each side, leaving the bean whole. Rinse clean and pat dry with paper towels. Set aside.

2. In a small bowl, combine sauce ingredients, mix well until dissolved and set aside.

3. In a wok or large frying pan, heat vegetable oil over high heat until hot. Stir-fry string beans until they begin to wrinkle, approximately 2–3 minutes. Remove from pan and drain oil.

4. In a clean wok or frying pan, heat 2 Tbs. vegetable oil over high heat. Add garlic and ginger root and cook for a few seconds until fragrant. Add string beans and sauce to pan and mix well until hot. Remove from heat and serve.

Vegetable Stir Fry with Noodles

(4–6 servings)

I included this recipe because it was a top selling vegetarian dish on our carry-out menu and I knew our customers would want to know how to make it. It is so simple to make, and includes several healthy vegetables which appeal to many people. This dish is oh so satisfying to eat!

1½ lb. to 2 lb. lo mein noodles
1½ cup sugar snap peas
1 cup carrots (shredded)
1 cup celery (shredded)
3–4 scallion stalks (cut into 2-inch pieces)
2 cups bean sprouts
3 Tbs. vegetable oil

Marinade

½ cup vegetable broth
½ tsp. white pepper
½ Tbs. salt
4 Tbs. soy sauce

1. In a small bowl, combine marinade ingredients, mix well and set aside.
2. Rinse bean sprouts until clean.
3. Fill a medium pot ¾ full with hot water and bring to a boil. Add lo mein noodles and cook until done (approximately 4 minutes) or according to package instructions. Remove from water and set aside in a bowl.
4. In a wok or large frying pan, heat 3 Tbs. vegetable oil over high heat until hot. Add carrots, celery, and sugar snap peas and stir-fry until hot (approximately 30–60 seconds).
5. Add noodles and mix well. Add marinade and bean sprouts. Stir-fry until very hot.
6. Finish with scallions, mix well. Remove from heat and serve.

You're gonna love it!

CPSIA information can be obtained at www.ICGtesting.com
Printed in the USA
BVIW12n2211290818
525651BV00036B/53